HEART HEALTHY

for beginners

Mallory Gross

Table of contents

HEART HEALTHY
FREE BONUS..6

THANK YOU!..7

BREAKFAST RECIPES 9

Artichokes creamy omelet 11

Avocado almond and pistachio
cheesy pancake 13

Banana and honey pancake............................15

Cheesy kale scrambled eggs 17

Peach hazelnut and berries yogurt bowl 19

Pineapple and mango yogurt
breakfast bowl 21

Rice cocoa and honey pancake 23

Strawberry and avocado toast 25

Tofu and avocado omelet...............................27

Zucchini and tuna scrambled eggs 29

LUNCH RECIPES 31

Black cabbage and walnuts
roasted turkey 33

Cashew and low-fat cheese

stuffed peppers 35

Chicken and peppers parsley Black rice............ 37

Fennel and basil cod 39

Green tea and ginger clam soup 41

Peppers and orange halibut.............................. 43

Steamed herbs salmon
and cucumbers mint salad................................ 45

Scallops and zucchini rice 47

Spicy chicken and shallot stew 49

Spinach and avocado tofu cream...................... 51

DINNER RECIPES.. 53

Cabbage and pumpkin sage oil black rice 55

Celery and Carrots chicken 57

Low fat cheese and tomato
stuffed pepper.. 59

Mackerel with potato cream
and coriander 61

Peas and mushroom cod stew........................... 63

Pecans and turmeric zucchini cream.................. 65

Rocket and cherry tomatoes halibut.................. 67

Tofu with broccoli cherry tomatoes
and pecans.. 69

Tofu and sweet potato stuffed eggplant 71

Tuna mushroom and radicchio salad................. 73

DESSERT RECIPES 75

Almond and lemon cake 77

Apple cubes and honey tofu................................. 79

Blackberry and coconut pudding..................... 81

Cranberry and cottage cheesecake.................. 83

Crumbled almonds with raspberry
and yogurt 85

Nuts and pear pudding 87

Passion fruit and oat flakes
yogurt dessert 89

Peach and low-fat cheese cold cake................ 91

Tea and yogurt sauce mango............................ 93

Vanilla and cocoa panna cotta 95

SNACK RECIPES.. 97

Apricot and oat flakes yogurt 99

Banana and vanilla vegan smoothie.............. 101

Cocoa strawberry and yogurt snack............... 103

Mango and tuna hard-boiled eggs 105

Peach and ginger vegan smoothie.................. 107

Pineapple and low sodium
cooked ham croutons...................................... 109

Smoked salmon stuffed avocado 111

Turkey and dill omelet..................................... 113

Tofu and tomato-stuffed lettuce leaves 115

Yogurt pistachio and egg white muffins 117

28 DAYS MEAL PLAN..................................... 118

FREE BONUS

Discover the exclusive bonus ready for you!

You have purchased the cookbook, but inside
the bonus you will find THE GUIDE to managing it
and living a healthy, balanced life.

Learn how to manage your diet and what are
the best tips to live a healthy life without giving up
the pleasure of food.

Scan the QR CODE to access
the free bonus, you will receive it immediately
ready to download!

WHAT TO DO NOW?

Show everyone the recipes you have prepared!

Take a photo or video of your recipes
and book and show everyone how you are
taking charge of your life!

Scan the QR CODE, upload the photo/video
and you're done!

Your input is essential to continuously
improve the content of my books; the opinions
of my readers are lifeblood to me.

Thank you very much in advance

BREAKFAST
RECIPES

ARTICHOKES CREAMY OMELET

PREPARATION TIME: 30 minutes

SERVINGS: 2

INGREDIENTS

→ 3 eggs
→ ½ cup of artichokes hearts
→ 1 tsp of olive oil
→ 1 pinch of smoked paprika
→ 2 tbsp of low-fat white yogurt
→ 1 tsp of chopped coriander
→ A pinch of salt

DIRECTIONS

1. Start with the artichoke's heart.
2. Remove the earthy part and wash them. After this operation, dry them and cut them into thin slices.
3. Put the 3 eggs in a bowl and beat them vigorously with a fork.
4. Add a pinch of salt and smoked paprika then combine all the ingredients well.
5. In a pan, sauté a drizzle of olive oil.
6. Once it is hot, sauté the artichokes for 9/10 minutes. Season with pepper and put them on a plate.
7. Takes an anti-adherent non-stick pan. When the pan will be very hot, add a little beaten egg.
8. Cook for 2/3 minutes on each side and then add a little artichoke and the yogurt.
9. Close the omelet, cook for another minute on each side and place it on a serving dish.
10. Repeat the operation until all the eggs are gone.
11. Meanwhile, wash and chop parsley.
12. Serve hot, sprinkled with chopped parsley.

NUTRITIONAL VALUES:

Calories	Protein	Carbs	Fat	Fiber	Sodium	Sugar	Cholesterol
123	8 gr	6 gr	6 gr	2 gr	150 mg	3 gr	171 mg

AVOCADO ALMOND AND PISTACHIO CHEESY PANCAKE

PREPARATION TIME: 15 minutes

SERVINGS: 2

INGREDIENTS

→ 4 tbsp of almond flour
→ 1 tbsp of finely chopped pistachios and 2tsp for final decoration
→ ½ avocado
→ 4 tbsp of coconut milk
→ A pinch of baking soda
→ 2 tbsp of low creamy cheese
→ Olive oil to taste

DIRECTIONS

1. Start by peeling, removing the central stone and slicing half the avocado.
2. Then put avocado slices in a mix and blend until obtaining a thick cream.
3. Add the coconut milk and beat with a whisk.
4. Then add the almond flour, 1 tbsp of chopped pistachios and baking soda.
5. Mix these ingredients until they will be smooth.
6. Then whip the egg whites until stiff and gently incorporate them into the rest of the avocado and nuts dough.
7. Heat a non-stick pan, and grease it lightly and pour a spoonful of avocado pancake dough and wait about a minute.
8. When the first bubbles form, you can turn avocado pancakes over and continue cooking on the other side.
9. Continue to cook all the avocado and almond pancakes like this.
10. Serve the avocado, pistachio, and almond pancakes still hot with a topping of low-fat creamy cheese and chopped pistachios.

NUTRITIONAL VALUES:

Calories	Protein	Carbs	Fat	Fiber	Sodium	Sugar	Cholesterol
240	7 gr	7 gr	18 gr	4 gr	38 mg	3 gr	2 mg

BANANA AND HONEY PANCAKE

PREPARATION TIME: 15 minutes

SERVINGS: 2

INGREDIENTS

→ ¼ Cup of wholemeal flour
→ ½ banana
→ 1 tbsp of soy milk
→ 1 tsp of lemon juice
→ A pinch of baking soda
→ 2 tsp of raw honey
→ Olive oil to taste

DIRECTIONS

1. Start this recipe by peeling and slicing the half banana.
2. Now, put banana slices in a mix and blend until obtaining a very thick cream.
3. Add 1 tsp of lemon juice to this banana cream and beat with a whisk.
4. Add the soy milk and beat again.
5. Then add the wholemeal flour and a pinch of baking soda.
6. Mix until all the ingredients will be smooth.
7. Then whip the egg whites until they will result stiff and gently incorporate them into the rest of the banana pancake dough.
8. Heat a non-stick pan and grease it very lightly.
9. Pour a spoonful of banana dough into each pancake and wait about a minute.
10. Once the first bubbles form, you can turn them over and continue cooking banana pancakes on the other side.
11. Keep on cooking all the banana pancakes like this.
12. Serve the banana pancakes still hot with a topping of raw honey.

NUTRITIONAL VALUES:

Calories	Protein	Carbs	Fat	Fiber	Sodium	Sugar	Cholesterol
180	4 gr	37 gr	3 gr	5 gr	7 mg	14 gr	0 mg

CHEESY KALE SCRAMBLED EGGS

PREPARATION TIME: 10 minutes

SERVINGS: 2

INGREDIENTS

→ 2 eggs
→ ½ cup of kale leaves
→ 2 tbsp of low-fat creamy cheese
→ 1 tsp olive oil
→ A pinch of salt

DIRECTIONS

1. First, wash and dry the kale leaves, then chop.
2. Take a non-stick pan and heat 1 tsp of oil.
3. When it is hot, add the chopped kale and brown it for 4 minutes, seasoning with a pinch of salt.
4. Let sauté for another 2 minutes.
5. In a dish, lightly beat the 2 eggs and after 5 minutes of kale, cooking put the eggs in the pan with the veggies.
6. Add the low-fat cream cheese cut into pieces and stir constantly so that the eggs divide into several separate pieces.
7. Cook for another 4/5 minutes and then put the eggs in a serving dish.
8. Serve your breakfast still hot.

NUTRITIONAL VALUES:

Calories	Protein	Carbs	Fat	Fiber	Sodium	Sugar	Cholesterol
91	6 gr	5 gr	5 gr	2 gr	120 mg	2 gr	100 mg

PEACH HAZELNUT AND BERRIES YOGURT BOWL

PREPARATION TIME: 15 minutes

SERVINGS: 2

INGREDIENTS

→ 1 ripe peach
→ 1 cup and ½ of low-fat Greek yogurt
→ 1 cup of mixed berries
→ 2 tsp of chopped hazelnuts

DIRECTIONS

1. First, peel the peach, remove the stone, and cut it into pieces.
2. Wash and dry the mixed berries cut 1/2 in half and ½ cup in thin slices.
3. Put the peach, low Greek yogurt and mixed berries cut in half in the blender glass.
4. Operate the blender and blend until you have obtained a thick and homogeneous mixture.
5. Now divide the mixture into two bowls.
6. First put the sliced berries on top, then the chopped hazelnuts and serve these bowls for breakfast.

NUTRITIONAL VALUES:

Calories	Protein	Carbs	Fat	Fiber	Sodium	Sugar	Cholesterol
200	8 gr	29 gr	3 gr	7 gr	70 mg	22 gr	30 mg

PINEAPPLE AND MANGO YOGURT BREAKFAST BOWL

PREPARATION TIME: 10 minutes

SERVINGS: 2

INGREDIENTS

→ 2 pots of low-fat white yogurt
→ 1 cup of pineapple pulp
→ 1 ripe mango
→ 2 tsp of raw honey

DIRECTIONS

1. First, peel and wash the ripe mango.
2. Remove the central stone and cut the mango into slices.
3. Wash and dry 1 cup of pineapple pulp and then cut them into slices too.
4. Put the low-fat yogurt in two bowls and then alternately put the mango and pineapple slices on top.
5. Sprinkle with raw honey and serve.

NUTRITIONAL VALUES:

Calories	Protein	Carbs	Fat	Fiber	Sodium	Sugar	Cholesterol
140	4 gr	32 gr	2 gr	3 gr	57 mg	26 gr	2 mg

RICE COCOA AND HONEY PANCAKE

PREPARATION TIME: 15 minutes

SERVINGS: 2

INGREDIENTS

- ¼ cup of rice flour
- 1 tbsp of no sugar cocoa powder
- 1 tbsp of raw honey
- 3 tbsp of low-fat white yogurt
- 1 pinch of cinnamon
- 1 tbsp of cane sugar
- 2 tbsp of rice milk
- 1 pinch of baking soda
- Olive oil to taste

DIRECTIONS

1. First, put the low-fat white yogurt in a large bowl and beat it with a whisk.
2. Add the rice milk too and honey, then beat again.
3. Then add the rice flour, cane sugar, cocoa powder, baking soda and ground cinnamon.
4. Let mix until all the ingredients will be very smooth.
5. Then whip the egg whites until stiff and carefully incorporate them into the rest of the cocoa and rice dough.
6. Heat a non-stick pan and grease it lightly, then pour a spoonful of dough for each rice honey and cocoa pancake and wait about a minute.
7. Once the first bubbles form, you can turn them over and continue cooking rice pancakes on the other side.
8. Continue to cook all the rice pancakes like this.
9. Serve these rice cocoa and honey pancakes still hot.

NUTRITIONAL VALUES:

Calories	Protein	Carbs	Fat	Fiber	Sodium	Sugar	Cholesterol
200	12 gr	26 gr	5 gr	5 gr	17 mg	14 gr	0 mg

STRAWBERRY AND AVOCADO TOAST

PREPARATION TIME: 15 minutes

SERVINGS: 2

INGREDIENTS

→ 4 little slices of wholemeal bread
→ ½ avocado
→ ½ cup of strawberries
→ 1 tbsp of marble syrup
→ 2 tbsp of lime juice
→ Olive oil to taste
→ A pinch of salt

DIRECTIONS

1. First, peel the half avocado. Remove the stone, cut it into small pieces and put it in a bowl.
2. Crush the avocado with a fork and then season it with oil, lime juice and salt.
3. Peel and wash the strawberries and then cut them into thin slices.
4. Season with the other tbsp of lime juice and marble syrup.
5. Put the slices of bread in the toaster and toast them until they are well crispy outside.
6. Once the bread is cooked, put it in two serving dishes and spread the avocado cream on the surface.
7. Put the slices of strawberries on top.
8. Serve these breakfast toasts.

NUTRITIONAL VALUES:

Calories	Protein	Carbs	Fat	Fiber	Sodium	Sugar	Cholesterol
240	7 gr	35 gr	6 gr	5 gr	190 mg	18 gr	0 mg

TOFU AND AVOCADO OMELET

PREPARATION TIME: 20 minutes

SERVINGS: 2

INGREDIENTS

- 2 little eggs
- 3 tbsp of diced tofu
- 1 tsp of olive oil
- 1 pinch of chili powder
- ½ avocado
- A pinch of salt

DIRECTIONS

1. Start with clearing the half avocado.
2. Remove the central stone, wash, dry and cut the pulp into cubes.
3. Rinse and
4. Put the 2 eggs in a bowl and beat them vigorously with a fork.
5. Add a pinch of salt and chili powder then mix the ingredients very well.
6. Add dice tofu.
7. Take a non-stick pan and heat a tsp of oil and then add a little beaten egg.
8. Cook for 2/3 minutes on each side.
9. Put the diced tofu inside and close the omelet, cook for another minute on each side and place it on a serving dish.
10. Place them with cubed avocado pulp in a dish and season with olive oil.
11. Serve your tofu omelet with avocado.

NUTRITIONAL VALUES:

Calories	Protein	Carbs	Fat	Fiber	Sodium	Sugar	Cholesterol
130	5 gr	1.5 gr	8 gr	1 gr	53 mg	0 gr	80 mg

ZUCCHINI AND TUNA SCRAMBLED EGGS

PREPARATION TIME: 20 minutes

SERVINGS: 2

INGREDIENTS

→ 2 eggs
→ 1 small size zucchini
→ ¼ cup of water
→ ¼ cup of low sodium drained tuna
→ 1 pinch of smoked paprika
→ 1 teaspoon of fresh chopped dill
→ 1 tsp of olive oil
→ A pinch of Salt

DIRECTIONS

1. Start by peeling and washing small size zucchini.
2. Cut the zucchini into little slices.
3. Take a non-stick pan and heat a very bit of oil.
4. When hot, add the zucchini and brown it for 3/4 minutes, seasoning with a pinch of salt and smoked paprika.
5. Add ¼ cup of water and let cook for another 10 minutes or until water will be absorbed.
6. Let zucchini drain well.
7. In a dish, lightly beat the eggs and after the zucchini is cooking time, put the eggs in the pan with zucchini slices.
8. Add drained tuna and stir constantly so that the eggs are in many separate pieces.
9. Cook for 4/5 minutes and then place the zucchini and tuna eggs into a serving dish.
10. Wash and chop the dill.
11. Serve your breakfast hot sprinkled with chopped dill.

NUTRITIONAL VALUES:

Calories	Protein	Carbs	Fat	Fiber	Sodium	Sugar	Cholesterol
145	3 gr	5 gr	7 gr	1 gr	60 mg	3 gr	105 mg

LUNCH RECIPES

BLACK CABBAGE AND WALNUTS ROASTED TURKEY

PREPARATION TIME: 25 minutes

SERVINGS: 2

INGREDIENTS

→ 2 slices of turkey breast of 0.44 lbs for each
→ 1 cup of black cabbage leaves
→ ½ red onion
→ 4 Walnut kernels
→ Olive oil to taste
→ A pinch of salt and pepper

DIRECTIONS

1. As the first step, wash and dab the turkey with a paper towel and then cut it into strips.
2. Peel and wash the red onion and then chop it.
3. Wash and dry the black cabbage leaves and then chop them.
4. Put a tablespoon of olive oil in a pan and then add the red onion.
5. Brown it for a couple of minutes and then put the turkey.
6. Sauté for 5 minutes, season with salt and pepper and then remove it and keep it aside.
7. Put the black cabbage now in the same pan.
8. Cook for 5 minutes, then season with a pinch of salt and pepper.
9. Take the turkey now and put it back in the pan with the black cabbage. Keep on cooking for another 5/6 minutes.
10. In the meantime, chop the 4 walnuts.
11. As soon as the turkey has finished cooking, turn it off and distribute it on the plates, together with the black cabbage leaves.
12. Sprinkle the turkey and cabbage with chopped walnuts and serve.

NUTRITIONAL VALUES:

Calories	Protein	Carbs	Fat	Fiber	Sodium	Sugar	Cholesterol
256	51 gr	6 gr	9 gr	4 gr	120 mg	1 gr	60 mg

CASHEW AND LOW-FAT CHEESE STUFFED PEPPERS

PREPARATION TIME: 30 minutes

SERVINGS: 2

INGREDIENTS

→ 4 long bell peppers
→ 1/3 cup of low-fat cream cheese
→ 2 tbsp of chopped cashews
→ 1 tsp of olive oil
→ 1 tbsp of oat flour
→ 1 slice of wholemeal bread
→ Salt and pepper to taste

DIRECTIONS

1. As the first step, preheat the oven to 392°F.
2. In the meantime, clean the peppers.
3. Wash the peppers and remove the top cap; also remove all seeds and white filaments inside.
4. Prepare the inside by putting in a blender the wholemeal bread, the oat flour, a tsp of oil and a pinch of salt and pepper.
5. Mix everything by blending.
6. Chop the cashews
7. Cut the low-fat cream cheese into small pieces as well.
8. Using a teaspoon, add the freshly chopped cashews and the oat and bread filling.
9. Also add the pieces of cream cheese.
10. Place the stuffed peppers in a baking dish lined with parchment paper and cook in the hot oven for about 20 minutes (or until they become soft and slightly darker).
11. Serve your peppers stuffed with cheese and cashews while still hot.

NUTRITIONAL VALUES:

Calories	Protein	Carbs	Fat	Fiber	Sodium	Sugar	Cholesterol
290	12 gr	19 gr	9 gr	5 gr	297 mg	6 gr	20 mg

CHICKEN AND PEPPERS PARSLEY BLACK RICE

PREPARATION TIME: 40 minutes

SERVINGS: 2

INGREDIENTS

- → ½ cup of black rice
- → ½ cup of chicken breast
- → A small shallot
- → 1 small yellow pepper
- → 2 cups of low sodium vegetable broth
- → 1 tsp of ginger powder
- → 1 tsp of smoked paprika
- → a glass of water
- → 1 teaspoon of chopped parsley
- → Olive oil to taste
- → A pinch of salt and pepper

DIRECTIONS

1. Start by putting the vegetable stock to a boil and then cook the black rice for 25 minutes about.
2. In the meantime, wash the chicken breast, dab it with a paper towel and then cut it into cubes.
3. Remove the cap, seeds and white filaments in the yellow pepper and then wash it and cut it into cubes.
4. Peel the small shallot, wash it, and then chop it.
5. Start a tablespoon of olive oil in a pan and freshly hot, and put the chopped shallot to brown.
6. Add the yellow pepper, mix, and cook for 5 minutes.
7. Now add the ginger, paprika and a glass of water and cook for another 2 minutes.
8. Add the chicken cubes, season with salt and pepper and continue cooking for 10 minutes.
9. As soon as the chicken is cooked, turn it off and set aside.
10. At this point, the cooking of the rice will be completed.
11. Drain it and put it in the pan with the chicken.
12. Mix to mix well and then transfer the rice to serving dishes.
13. Sprinkle with the parsley and serve.

NUTRITIONAL VALUES:

Calories	Protein	Carbs	Fat	Fiber	Sodium	Sugar	Cholesterol
337	22 gr	48 gr	6 gr	3 gr	205 mg	1 gr	56 mg

FENNEL AND BASIL COD

PREPARATION TIME: 30 minutes

SERVINGS: 2

INGREDIENTS

→ 2 cups of cod fillets
→ 1 table fennel
→ 1 tsp of chopped basil
→ 1 orange
→ Olive oil to taste
→ A pinch of salt and pepper

DIRECTIONS

1. The first step, start with the fennel.
2. Remove the beard, separate the various leaves, wash them under running water, dry them and then cut the fennel into slices.
3. Also wash some tufts of beard and set them aside.
4. Take a pan and heat half 1 tsp of oil.
5. Let the oil heat up and then put the fennel slices for about ten minutes to sauté, adding salt and a drop of water.
6. Now switch to the cod fillets.
7. Remove all bones inside and wash them under running water and dry them.
8. Now take a pan and put two sheets of parchment paper inside the pan.
9. Grease the parchment paper with a little oil, add the cod fillets, and a pinch of salt, sprinkle it with pepper and sprinkle everything with the orange juice and a drizzle of olive oil and the fennel beard that you had set aside.
10. Put the tuna to cook in a preheated oven at 338° F for about 20 minutes.
11. As soon as they are ready, remove the cod fillets from the parchment paper, remove the fennel barbette and place the cod in a serving dish surrounded by the previously cooked fennel.
12. Serve with the washed and chopped basil sprinkled on top.

NUTRITIONAL VALUES:

Calories	Protein	Carbs	Fat	Fiber	Sodium	Sugar	Cholesterol
195	34 gr	7 gr	3 gr	2 gr	400 mg	4 gr	94 mg

GREEN TEA AND GINGER CLAM SOUP

PREPARATION TIME: 30 minutes

SERVINGS: 2

INGREDIENTS

→ 1.1. lbs of clams
→ 2 medium -sized zucchinis
→ 1 shallot
→ ½ cup of peeled tomato
→ 2 cups of low sodium vegetable stock
→ 2 tbsp of powdered green tea
→ 1 tbsp of powdered ginger
→ Olive oil to taste
→ A pinch of salt and pepper

DIRECTIONS

1. Start this soup recipe with the cleaning of the clams, which must be in a basin with water and salt all night.
2. When it's time to cook clams, drain them and put them in a pan, so that they open.
3. As soon as they have opened, turn off, put them in a bowl and filter the cooking juice in another bowl.
4. Wash the zucchinis and then cut them into thin slices.
5. Peel and wash the shallot, then chop.
6. Heat a spoonful of oil in a pan and just hot, brown the chopped shallot.
7. As soon as it is golden brown, put the zucchinis and peeled tomato.
8. Cook for 5 minutes, add the clams and mix.
9. Now, add the scallops cooking bottom juice, broth, green tea, and ginger powder.
10. Stir, season with a pinch of salt and pepper, and proceed with cooking for another 10 minutes.
11. As soon as the soup is ready, turn off and immediately put it on the serving dishes.
12. Season with a drop of raw oil and serve.

NUTRITIONAL VALUES:

Calories	Protein	Carbs	Fat	Fiber	Sodium	Sugar	Cholesterol
240	40 gr	17 gr	5 gr	4 gr	201 mg	9 gr	56 mg

PEPPERS AND ORANGE HALIBUT

PREPARATION TIME: 30 minutes

SERVINGS: 2

INGREDIENTS

- → 2 cups of cleaned Halibut fillets
- → 1 sprig of rosemary
- → 1 small orange
- → 1 small yellow pepper
- → 1 small red pepper
- → Olive oil to taste
- → A pinch of salt and Pepper

DIRECTIONS

1. Wash and dry the halibut fillet, then cut it into thin strips.
2. Wash and dry the rosemary, take the needles, and then chop them finely.
3. Remove the cap, seeds, and lateral filaments from both peppers and then cut them into strips.
4. Heat 1 tsp of olive oil in a pan.
5. Once it is hot, sauté the peppers for 5 minutes.
6. After 5 minutes, add the halibut strips and rosemary.
7. Cook for 10 minutes and then sprinkle everything with the squeezed orange juice.
8. Continue cooking for another 5 minutes, season with a pinch of salt and pepper and then turn off.
9. Put the halibut with orange peppers on serving dishes, sprinkle with the cooking juice and serve.

NUTRITIONAL VALUES:

Calories	Protein	Carbs	Fat	Fiber	Sodium	Sugar	Cholesterol
290	44 gr	13 gr	5 gr	4 gr	236 mg	7 gr	94 mg

STEAMED HERBS SALMON AND CUCUMBERS MINT SALAD

PREPARATION TIME: 30 minutes

SERVINGS: 2

INGREDIENTS

→ 0.66 lbs of salmon fillet
→ 2 small size cucumbers
→ 4 mint leaves
→ 1 sprig of marjoram
→ 3 cups of water
→ 1 sprig of rosemary
→ 1 sage leaf
→ Apple cider vinegar to taste
→ Olive oil to taste
→ A pinch of salt and pepper

DIRECTIONS

1. Remove the bones and skin from the salmon fillet. Proceed with washing and drying the fish fillet.
2. Wash marjoram, rosemary, and sage leaf.
3. Put 3 cups of water in a pot together with the aromatic herbs and boiled.
4. Add the salmon, salt and pepper and cook for 10 minutes.
5. After 10 minutes, drain and let it cool.
6. In the meantime, wash and dry the mint leaves and then chop them.
7. Put the mint in a bowl together with a spoonful of olive oil, one of apple cider vinegar, salt and pepper and mix.
8. Wash the cucumbers and then cut them into slices.
9. Cut the salmon into cubes now.
10. Put the salmon and cucumber in a salad bowl and mix.
11. Sprinkle with mint emulsion and serve.

NUTRITIONAL VALUES:

Calories	Protein	Carbs	Fat	Fiber	Sodium	Sugar	Cholesterol
300	34 gr	3 gr	11 gr	1 gr	170 mg	1 gr	83 mg

SCALLOPS AND ZUCCHINI RICE

PREPARATION TIME: 45 minutes

SERVINGS: 2

INGREDIENTS

→ ½ cup of black rice
→ 1 cup of shelled and cleaned scallops
→ ½ cup of zucchini
→ 1 garlic clove
→ 1 tbsp of chopped thyme
→ Olive oil to taste
→ Salt and pepper to taste

DIRECTIONS

1. Start the preparation with the cooking of black rice.
2. Put water and salt in a pot and bring to a boil. Pour the rice and cook for 25 minutes, or following the times shown in the package.
3. In the meantime, take the already-shelled scallops then wash them and let them drain.
4. Peel the zucchini, wash them, and then cut them into cubes (1/2 cup).
5. Peel and wash the garlic and then chop it.
6. Put a tablespoon of olive oil in a pan, heat it and then put the garlic to brown.
7. As soon as it is golden brown, add the zucchini cubes.
8. Season with a pinch of salt and pepper, add the washed and chopped thyme mix and then cook for 5 minutes.
9. Add the scallops now, mix and continue cooking for another 5 minutes.
10. After 5 minutes, turn it off and set it aside.
11. As soon as the rice is cooked, drain it and transfer it to the pan with the prawns.
12. Mix to flavor the rice well and then put it on serving dishes and serve.

NUTRITIONAL VALUES:

Calories	Protein	Carbs	Fat	Fiber	Sodium	Sugar	Cholesterol
490	21 gr	48 gr	3 gr	6 gr	480 mg	1 gr	50 mg

SPICY CHICKEN AND SHALLOT STEW

PREPARATION TIME: 45 minutes

SERVINGS: 2

INGREDIENTS

- 2 cups of chicken breast
- 1 cup of peeled tomatoes
- 1 shallot
- 1 chopped chili pepper
- 1tsp of smoked paprika
- 1 tbsp of chopped dill
- ¼ cup of water
- Salt and pepper to taste
- Olive oil to taste

DIRECTIONS

1. As the first step, wash and dry the chicken breast, remove the excess fat, and then cut it into cubes.
2. Peel the shallot, wash it, and chop it.
3. Put a spoonful of oil in a pot and just hot and put the chopped shallot to brown.
4. After a couple of minutes, put the chicken cubes to sauté.
5. Mix them a flavor for 3 minutes and then add salt, pepper, smoked paprika and chili pepper.
6. Mix and after 2 minutes add the peeled tomato and ¼ cup of water.
7. Cook for 20 minutes, stirring occasionally.
8. When everything will be cooked, put the chicken and shallot stew on the plates, sprinkle with the chopped dill and serve.

NUTRITIONAL VALUES:

Calories	Protein	Carbs	Fat	Fiber	Sodium	Sugar	Cholesterol
320	52 gr	7 gr	6 gr	2 gr	200 mg	3 gr	64 mg

SPINACH AND AVOCADO TOFU CREAM

PREPARATION TIME: 20 minutes

SERVINGS: 2

INGREDIENTS

- ½ cup of tofu cheese
- 1 small avocado
- 1/3 cup of fresh baby spinach leaves
- a shallot
- 1 tsp of Olive
- 1 tsp of apple cider vinegar
- 1 tsp of chopped dill
- A pinch of salt and pepper

DIRECTIONS

1. As the first step, drain the tofu and then cut it into cubes.
2. Wash and chop spinach leaves.
3. Peel the small avocado, removing the central core and then cut it into cubes.
4. Peel and wash the shallot and then chop it.
5. Start a tablespoon of olive oil in a pan, then brown the shallot for a couple of minutes.
6. Add the tofu and spinach leaves now, season with salt and pepper and mix.
7. Add a couple of tablespoons of water and cook for 5 minutes.
8. After 5 minutes, add the avocado cubes and apple cider vinegar.
9. Cook for another 10 minutes, stirring occasionally.
10. After 10 minutes, turn off, and blend everything with an immersion blender.
11. Pour the cream obtained onto serving dishes.
12. Sprinkle with the chopped dill and serve.

NUTRITIONAL VALUES:

Calories	Protein	Carbs	Fat	Fiber	Sodium	Sugar	Cholesterol
170	8 gr	7 gr	16 gr	4 gr	45 mg	3 gr	0 mg

DINNER RECIPES

PUMPKIN SAGE OIL BLACK RICE

PREPARATION TIME: 45 minutes

SERVINGS: 2

INGREDIENTS

→ ½ cup and 1 tbsp of black rice
→ 4 cups of low sodium vegetable broth
→ ½ cup of green cabbage leaves
→ ½ cup of pumpkin pulp
→ 1 garlic clove
→ 2 sage leaves
→ Olive oil to taste
→ A pinch of salt and pepper

DIRECTIONS

1. As the first operation, wash and dry the sage and place them in a bowl coated with oil.
2. Divide the green cabbage leaves, wash them, and then cut them into small pieces.
3. Peel the garlic clove and chop it.
4. Wash the pumpkin pulp and then cut it into cubes.
5. Put a drizzle of olive oil in a pan, and fry the chopped garlic for a minute.
6. Stir and after 2 minutes add the pumpkin cubes.
7. After two minutes, add the rice, stir, season with a pinch of salt and pepper and add 4 cups of broth.
8. Cook for about twenty minutes, or until the black rice is soft.
9. Add the green cabbage and cook for another 2 minutes.
10. Adjust if you need salt and pepper and then put the black rice and vegetables on the serving plates.
11. Sprinkle the plates with a teaspoon each of sage oil and serves.

NUTRITIONAL VALUES:

Calories	Protein	Carbs	Fat	Fiber	Sodium	Sugar	Cholesterol
285	9 gr	53 gr	4 gr	4 gr	325 mg	5 gr	0 mg

CELERY AND CARROTS CHICKEN

PREPARATION TIME: 35 minutes

SERVINGS: 2

INGREDIENTS

→ 0.66 lbs of already cleaned chicken breast
→ 2 small carrots
→ 1 stick of celery
→ ½ white onion
→ 3 tbsp of tomato puree
→ 1 tsp of dried thyme
→ 1 glass of water
→ Olive oil to taste
→ A pinch of salt and pepper

DIRECTIONS

1. First, peel the half-white onion, wash it, and then chop it.
2. Remove the celery stalk, and the white filaments and then wash it and cut it into small pieces.
3. Take the carrots, peel them, wash them, and then cut them into cubes.
4. Wash and dry the chicken breast.
5. In a pan, heat a drizzle of olive oil.
6. As soon as it is hot, sauté the onion for a couple of minutes.
7. Now add the celery and carrot and mix.
8. Cook for 2 minutes and then add the chicken breast.
9. Stir, season with salt and pepper and then add the tomato puree and thyme.
10. Add a glass of water, cover with a lid, and cook for 20 minutes about.
11. 11.As soon as it is ready, place the chicken with carrots on serving plates and serve immediately.

NUTRITIONAL VALUES:

Calories	Protein	Carbs	Fat	Fiber	Sodium	Sugar	Cholesterol
396	52 gr	23 gr	9 gr	6 gr	260 mg	11 gr	137 mg

LOW FAT CHEESE AND TOMATO STUFFED PEPPER

PREPARATION TIME: 40 minutes

SERVINGS: 2

INGREDIENTS

→ 2 bell peppers
→ ½ cup of diced low-fat cheese
→ 2 tomatoes
→ 1 tsp of chopped mint
→ ½ shallot
→ Olive oil to taste
→ A pinch of salt and pepper

DIRECTIONS

1. First, wash and dry the 2 tomatoes and then cut them into cubes.
2. Remove the stone, filaments, and seeds from the peppers, cut them in half, wash them and then empty them by removing the inner part.
3. Peel and wash the half shallot.
4. Wash and dry the mint leaves, then chop.
5. Put the shallot and mint in the glass of the mixer and then blend.
6. Now add the inside of the pepper, a little oil, salt and pepper and the diced low-fat cheese.
7. Blend again until you get a smooth and homogeneous mixture.
8. Take a baking pan and brush it with olive oil. Put the boat of peppers inside.
9. Fill the peppers with the mint low fat cheese mixture and then sprinkle them with the tomato cubes.
10. Bake the peppers in the oven at 338°F for 30 minutes.
11. When peppers are cooked, take them out of the oven. Then put them on serving plates and serve.

NUTRITIONAL VALUES:

Calories	Protein	Carbs	Fat	Fiber	Sodium	Sugar	Cholesterol
133	8 gr	24 gr	4 gr	4 gr	36 mg	7 gr	1 mg

MACKEREL WITH POTATO CREAM AND CORIANDER

PREPARATION TIME: 45 minutes

SERVINGS: 2

INGREDIENTS

→ 2 fillets of mackerel of 0.33 lbs for each
→ 2 medium sized potatoes
→ 1 tbsp of chopped onion
→ 2 tbsp of low-fat cooking cream
→ 1 sprig of thyme
→ 1 sprig of rosemary
→ 1 tsp of chopped coriander
→ 1 tsp of olive oil
→ A pinch of salt and pepper

DIRECTIONS

1. Start to prepare the cream by peeling the potatoes. After that, wash and dry them. Cut them into thin slices.
2. Wash and dry both the thyme and rosemary.
3. In a pan, heat 1 tsp of oil and then put 1 tbsp of chopped onion to fry together with thyme and rosemary. When the onion is golden brown, add the potato slices.
4. Sauté for a couple of minutes and season with salt and pepper. Cook the potatoes for 25/30 minutes.
5. Meanwhile, prepare the mackerel. Wash and dry the fish, remove the skin and bones, and cut the pulp into cubes.
6. Heat a drizzle of oil in a pan, add the mackerel and cook for about ten minutes. Remove from the heat and set the fish aside.
7. When the potatoes are soft enough, turn off, remove the thyme and rosemary and blend everything with an immersion blender.
8. Add the low-fat cooking cream and with a wooden spoon mix it with the potatoes.
9. Transfer the cream to a bowl, add the mackerel cubes and decorate with the washed and chopped coriander.

NUTRITIONAL VALUES:

Calories	Protein	Carbs	Fat	Fiber	Sodium	Sugar	Cholesterol
396	35 gr	37 gr	11 gr	4 gr	86 mg	3 gr	83 mg

PEAS AND MUSHROOM COD STEW

PREPARATION TIME: 25 minutes

SERVINGS: 2

INGREDIENTS

- → 2 cups of cod fillet
- → 1 cup of fresh peas
- → 1 large ripe tomato
- → A sprig of parsley
- → ½ cup of champignon mushrooms
- → 1 glass of water
- → Olive oil to taste
- → A pinch of salt and pepper

DIRECTIONS

1. First, remove the bones, and the skin and clean the cod fillet.
2. Wash and dry the cod fillet and then cut it into cubes.
3. Remove the earthy part of the champignon mushrooms, wash them, dry them, and cut them into slices.
4. Wash the tomato and then cut it into cubes.
5. Shell the peas, wash them and then drain them.
6. Put a little oil in a saucepan and brown the mushrooms and tomato.
7. Stir and then add the cod cubes.
8. Cook for 5 minutes and then add the peas. Add a glass of water and cook for 15 minutes.
9. Meanwhile, wash and dry the parsley and then chop it.
10. As soon as the cod and veggies stew is cooked, turn it off and add the chopped parsley.
11. Mix, mix well and then put on plates and serve this fish and veggies stew.

NUTRITIONAL VALUES:

Calories	Protein	Carbs	Fat	Fiber	Sodium	Sugar	Cholesterol
266	38 gr	22 gr	3 gr	7 gr	519 mg	9 gr	94 mg

PECANS AND TURMERIC ZUCCHINI CREAM

PREPARATION TIME: 30 minutes

SERVINGS: 2

INGREDIENTS

- → 2 small size zucchinis
- → 4 tsp of chopped pecans
- → 2 cups of water
- → 1 tsp of turmeric
- → ¼ tsp of chili powder
- → Olive oil to taste
- → A pinch of salt and pepper

DIRECTIONS

1. First, tick the zucchinis, wash them, and then cut them into small pieces.
2. Put a tsp of olive oil in a saucepan and let it heat up.
3. Add the zucchini, chili powder and turmeric and brown them for 5 minutes.
4. Add the chopped pecans, a pinch of salt and pepper and mix.
5. Now add 2 cups of water and keep on cooking for another 15 minutes.
6. After this cooking time, turn off the zucchinis and blend everything with an immersion blender, until you get a smooth and homogeneous mixture.
7. Put the zucchinis and pecans cream on plates, season with a drizzle of oil and serve.

NUTRITIONAL VALUES:

Calories	Protein	Carbs	Fat	Fiber	Sodium	Sugar	Cholesterol
108	3 gr	6 gr	8 gr	2 gr	3 mg	3 gr	0 mg

ROCKET AND CHERRY TOMATOES HALIBUT

PREPARATION TIME: 25 minutes

SERVINGS: 2

INGREDIENTS

- 0.66 lbs of halibut fillet
- 1 garlic clove
- ¼ cup of rocket salad
- ½ cup of cherry tomatoes
- Olive oil to taste
- A pinch of salt and pepper

DIRECTIONS

1. Remove the skin and central bone from the halibut. Wash and dry the halibut fillet and then cut it into strips.
2. Peel and wash the garlic clove.
3. Wash the rocket salad and then dry it.
4. Wash the cherry tomatoes and then halve them.
5. Start a tsp of oil in a pan and just hot brown the garlic.
6. As soon as the garlic is golden brown, remove it and put the halibut fillet in.
7. Sauté a couple of minutes and then add the cherry tomatoes.
8. Continue cooking for 3 minutes and then add the rocket salad.
9. Cook for another 3 minutes, season with salt and pepper and turn off.
10. Put the halibut strips, the cherry tomatoes and the rocket on the serving dishes and serve.

NUTRITIONAL VALUES:

Calories	Protein	Carbs	Fat	Fiber	Sodium	Sugar	Cholesterol
300	22 gr	5 gr	4 gr	1 gr	67 mg	2 gr	70 mg

TOFU WITH BROCCOLI CHERRY TOMATOES AND PECANS

PREPARATION TIME: 20 minutes

SERVINGS: 2

INGREDIENTS

- ½ broccoli already steamed or boiled
- 10 cherry tomatoes
- A pinch of chili powder
- 2 tbsp of chopped pecans
- ¼ cup of toasted and grated tofu
- 2 tsp of olive oil
- A pinch of salt and black pepper

DIRECTIONS

1. First, wash the cherry tomatoes and cut them in half.
2. In the meantime, mash the half broccoli directly in a baking dish; it doesn't have to become a puree just shrink in volume.
3. Season with grated tofu, cherry tomatoes, pepper, oil, and a pinch of chili powder.
4. Mix the ingredients well and season with salt.
5. Finally add the chopped pecans scattered over.
6. Stir again and cook in a preheated oven at 375° F for 15 minutes.
7. Serve the broccoli and tofu dish hot directly on serving plates.

NUTRITIONAL VALUES:

Calories	Protein	Carbs	Fat	Fiber	Sodium	Sugar	Cholesterol
186	8 gr	11 gr	10 gr	4 gr	40 mg	5 gr	0 mg

TOFU AND SWEET POTATO STUFFED EGGPLANT

PREPARATION TIME: 40 minutes

SERVINGS: 2

INGREDIENTS

→ 2 long eggplants
→ 1 cup of boiled sweet potato cubes
→ 1/3 cup of diced tofu
→ ¼ cup of low-fat soy cream
→ Olive oil to taste
→ A pinch of salt and pepper

DIRECTIONS

1. First, if you have not already done so, cut 1 cup of sweet potatoes into cubes and boil them for 15 minutes in boiling salted water.
2. In the meantime, cut the eggplants lengthwise, empty them and put them upside down to eliminate the bitter water.
3. Then wash and dry them well.
4. Heat the soy cream in a saucepan.
5. Cut the tofu into cubes and add to the soy cream, stirring constantly.
6. Let it harden then add the sweet potato cubes to the cream.
7. Fill the eggplants with this tofu and potato mixture.
8. Line a baking dish with parchment paper and place the stuffed eggplants in it, sprinkling them with a pinch of salt and pepper.
9. Bake in a preheated oven at 392° C and cook for 25/30 minutes.
10. Check the cooking and, if they are not yet cooked, continue for a few more minutes.
11. When cooked, serve the tofu and sweet potato stuffed eggplant still hot.

NUTRITIONAL VALUES:

Calories	Protein	Carbs	Fat	Fiber	Sodium	Sugar	Cholesterol
224	9 gr	38 gr	7 gr	10 gr	90 mg	12 gr	1 mg

TUNA MUSHROOM AND RADICCHIO SALAD

PREPARATION TIME: 30 minutes

SERVINGS: 2

INGREDIENTS

→ 1 cup of tuna fillet
→ 4 button mushrooms
→ ¼ cup of radicchio leaves
→ Apple cider vinegar to taste
→ Salt and pepper to taste
→ Olive oil to taste

DIRECTIONS

1. As the first step, wash and dry the tuna fillet and season it with salt and pepper.
2. Put it in a bustle brushed with olive oil and cook in the oven at 375°F for 10/12 minutes.
3. In the meantime, wash and dry the radicchio leaves, then chop very finely.
4. Remove the earthy part from the 4 button mushrooms, wash them, dry them, and then cut them into thin slices.
5. When the tuna fillet will be cooked, remove it from the oven and let it rest for 5 minutes.
6. Divide the radicchio and mushrooms into two serving dishes.
7. Cut the fillet into slices and put the vegetables on top.
8. Put a spoonful of oil in a bowl, two of apple cider vinegar, salt and pepper and mix.
9. Sprinkle the tuna mushrooms and radicchio with the emulsion and serve.

NUTRITIONAL VALUES:

Calories	Protein	Carbs	Fat	Fiber	Sodium	Sugar	Cholesterol
80	25 gr	8 gr	11 gr	2 gr	92 mg	4 gr	40 mg

DESSERT RECIPES

ALMOND AND LEMON CAKE

PREPARATION TIME: 20 minutes

SERVINGS: 2

INGREDIENTS

→ ½ cup of wholemeal flour
→ 2 tbsp of chopped almonds
→ 2 tbsp of cane sugar
→ 2 little eggs
→ 1 tbsp of grated lemon zest
→ 1 pinch of baking powder
→ 2 tbsp Lemon juice
→ 2 tsp of olive oil

DIRECTIONS

1. Start by putting the chopped almonds, wholemeal flour, cane sugar and a pinch of baking powder in a bowl.
2. Combine these cake ingredients well.
3. In a separate bowl, beat the 2 little eggs until they swell.
4. Add the lemon juice, olive oil, beaten eggs and lemon zest to the almond and wholemeal flour mixture.
5. Stir until all the ingredients are well blended.
6. Grease some baking cups with a little butter.
7. Spread the smoothing batter into the bowls.
8. Bake in the oven at 405°F for about 8/10 minutes.
9. Insert a toothpick and if it does not come out dry, bake for another maximum minute until cooked.
10. Serve the cake just warmed.

NUTRITIONAL VALUES:

Calories	Protein	Carbs	Fat	Fiber	Sodium	Sugar	Cholesterol
330	12 gr	48 gr	11 gr	7 gr	33 mg	11 gr	80 mg

APPLE CUBES AND HONEY TOFU

PREPARATION TIME: 30 minutes

SERVINGS: 2

INGREDIENTS

→ 0.35 lbs of tofu
→ 1 red apple
→ 2 tsp of honey
→ Olive oil to taste

DIRECTIONS

1. As the first step, rinse and pat the tofu with a paper towel and then cut it into cubes.
2. Peel the red apple, remove the core and seeds, and then cut it into cubes.
3. Heat a tsp of olive oil in a pan, then brown the tofu for a few minutes.
4. Add a couple of tablespoons of water and cook for 5 minutes.
5. After 5 minutes, add the apple cubes as well.
6. Cook for another 10 minutes and stirring occasionally.
7. After 10 minutes turn off, put your plate of tofu and apples on serving plates and serve with a honey topping.

NUTRITIONAL VALUES:

Calories	Protein	Carbs	Fat	Fiber	Sodium	Sugar	Cholesterol
176	7 gr	25 gr	7 gr	2 gr	6 mg	19 gr	0 mg

BLACKBERRY AND COCONUT PUDDING

PREPARATION TIME: 35 minutes

SERVINGS: 2

INGREDIENTS

→ 1 cup of blackberries
→ 1 tbsp of honey
→ 1 cup of coconut milk
→ 2 tbsp of coconut flour
→ 1 vanilla pod
→ The grated rind of one lemon.

DIRECTIONS

1. As the first step, wash the blackberries, cut them in half and let them dry.
2. Put the blackberries in a bowl and add the honey.
3. Stir and let it steep for about 30 minutes.
4. Put the coconut flour in a saucepan and add a little coconut milk at a time.
5. Stir with a manual whisk and, as soon as you have finished adding all the coconut milk, add the vanilla pod cut in half and the lemon zest.
6. Stir until you have obtained a thick and homogeneous mixture.
7. Now add the blackberries and continue mixing, until everything is well blended.
8. Now pour the mixture into two aluminum molds.
9. Let it cool completely.
10. Now cover the molds with cling film and then transfer them to the fridge.
11. Let them harden for 3 hours.
12. After 3 hours, remove the molds from the fridge.
13. Turn the puddings upside down on a serving dish and serve with a sprinkle of other coconut flour (optional).

NUTRITIONAL VALUES:

Calories	Protein	Carbs	Fat	Fiber	Sodium	Sugar	Cholesterol
236	11 gr	23 gr	10 gr	5 gr	106 mg	15 gr	25 mg

CRANBERRY AND COTTAGE CHEESECAKE

PREPARATION TIME: 45 minutes

SERVINGS: 2

INGREDIENTS

→ 1/3 cup of wholemeal flour
→ 2 tsp of raw honey
→ ¼ cup of coconut flour
→ ½ cup of unsweetened vegetable milk
→ ½ cup of low-fat cottage cheese
→ ½ cup egg white
→ The zest of 1 lemon
→ ½ tsp of baking powder
→ ½ cup of cranberries

DIRECTIONS

1. First, preheat the oven to 338° F.
2. Combine the two flours (wholemeal and coconut) with the baking powder.
3. Take care to mix them well so that they are then evenly distributed throughout the dough.
4. In another bowl, mix the egg white and low-fat cottage cheese, lightly whipping the mixture.
5. Also add the raw honey and the lemon zest, continuing to mix until you have obtained a frothy and homogeneous mixture.
6. At this point, you can combine the two flours a little at a time, continuing to mix.
7. the mixture will be very solid: then add the milk a little at a time until you get a consistency that is neither too liquid nor too hard (like donut dough).
8. Gently incorporate the washed and chopped cranberries into the dough.
9. Pour the cranberry cottage cheese and coconut mixture into the pan lined with parchment paper.
10. Bake the cake for about 35 minutes.
11. Always test the toothpick before taking it out.
12. If the cake is cooked, let it cool out of the oven
13. Serve this cottage cheese and cranberry as it has cooled completely.

NUTRITIONAL VALUES:

Calories	Protein	Carbs	Fat	Fiber	Sodium	Sugar	Cholesterol
410	15 gr	47 gr	13 gr	11 gr	90 mg	11 gr	26 mg

CRUMBLED ALMONDS WITH RASPBERRY AND YOGURT

PREPARATION TIME: 30 minutes

SERVINGS: 2

INGREDIENTS

→ 3 tbsp of almond flour
→ 1 tbsp of coconut oil
→ 1 tbsp of raw honey
→ 1 tbsp of sliced almonds
→ ½ cup of low-fat Greek yogurt
→ ¼ cup of raspberries
→ A pinch of salt

DIRECTIONS

1. Start this dessert recipe by preheating the oven to 338°F.
2. In a large bowl, combine the almond flour, honey, melted coconut oil, sliced almonds, and a pinch of salt.
3. Mix the ingredients with your hands until many grains have formed.
4. Pour the mixture into a baking tray covered with parchment paper and cook for 10 minutes, stirring the mixture from time to time to prevent it from burning.
5. In the meantime, move on to preparing the cake bases. Wash and dry the raspberries and then chop them into small pieces.
6. Put half of the low-fat Greek yogurt and raspberries in two glasses and then put them in the fridge to rest.
7. When the crumbled almonds are cooked, remove them from the oven and let them cool.
8. As soon as it is cold, take the glasses with the raspberries and low-fat yogurt from the fridge and sprinkle them with the almond crumble and then serve.

NUTRITIONAL VALUES:

Calories	Protein	Carbs	Fat	Fiber	Sodium	Sugar	Cholesterol
220	8 gr	19 gr	13 gr	5 gr	44 mg	13 gr	2 mg

NUTS AND PEAR PUDDING

PREPARATION TIME: 10 minutes

SERVINGS: 2

INGREDIENTS

- 1 pear cut into cubes
- 2 cups of unsweetened almond milk
- ¼ cup of mixed nuts
- 1 tbsp of raw honey
- 1 tbsp of orange juice

DIRECTIONS

1. Start by placing the almond milk and mixed chopped nuts in two glasses or two glass jars, alternating them.
2. Stir well several times with a spoon or a teaspoon to distribute them evenly in the vegetable milk.
3. Add the raw honey spoon.
4. Let the pudding rest for at least two hours before serving it in the fridge.
5. Meanwhile, peel the pear, wash it and remove the internal seeds.
6. Cut the pear into cubes and season with the orange juice
7. Serve your pudding with pear cubes as dessert.

NUTRITIONAL VALUES:

Calories	Protein	Carbs	Fat	Fiber	Sodium	Sugar	Cholesterol
368	10 gr	46 gr	12 gr	9 gr	96 mg	30 gr	0 mg

PASSION FRUIT AND OAT FLAKES YOGURT DESSERT

PREPARATION TIME: 10 minutes

SERVINGS: 2

INGREDIENTS

→ 1 cup of low-fat white yogurt
→ 1 Maracuja fruit (or passion fruit)
→ The grated rind of an orange
→ 2 tsp of powdered ginger
→ ¼ cup of oat flakes

DIRECTIONS

1. First wash and dry the passion fruit, removing the central seeds and cutting them into small pieces.
2. Put the pieces of passion fruit in a bowl and add the orange zest and powdered ginger.
3. Stir to flavor the passion fruit well.
4. Add the low-fat white yogurt and stir until the mixture is well blended.
5. Now put the mixture in two bowls.
6. Sprinkle with oat flakes and serve.

NUTRITIONAL VALUES:

Calories	Protein	Carbs	Fat	Fiber	Sodium	Sugar	Cholesterol
220	13 gr	30 gr	7 gr	6 gr	50 mg	20 gr	0 mg

PEACH AND LOW-FAT CHEESE COLD CAKE

PREPARATION TIME: 10 minutes

SERVINGS: 2

INGREDIENTS

→ 2 tbsp of melted soy butter

→ 2 tbsp of coconut oil

→ ¼ cup low fat cream cheese at room temperature

→ 1 tbsp of cane sugar

→ ¼ cup of cubed peach

→ 1 tsp of lime juice

DIRECTIONS

1. First, melt the soy butter in a low-power microwave-safe bowl.

2. Check it every 10-20 seconds because you will need to get a slightly warm melted butter. Stir it often, until it is completely dissolved.

3. Do the same process with coconut oil.

4. In a medium-sized bowl, pour the melted soy butter and coconut oil, add the low-fat cream cheese, and mix well.

5. Peel a peach, wash it, remove the stone, and take ¼ of the pulp. Cube peach pulp.

6. Add to the soy and coconut mixture the cane sugar, cubed peach pulp and lime juice.

7. Mix all the ingredients well.

8. Pour the mixture into small silicone molds and put them in the freezer for at least 2 hours, until the cakes have hardened.

9. To serve the mini raspberry cakes, take them out of the freezer 5 minutes before serving.

10. Remove them from the silicone molds and place them in a small tray, plate or small paper cup.

11. Serve these peach cakes cold.

NUTRITIONAL VALUES:

Calories	Protein	Carbs	Fat	Fiber	Sodium	Sugar	Cholesterol
135	4 gr	16 gr	6 gr	3.5 gr	10 mg	12 gr	0 mg

TEA AND YOGURT SAUCE MANGO

PREPARATION TIME: 60 minutes

SERVINGS: 2

INGREDIENTS

→ 2 ripe mangoes
→ 1 cup and ½ water
→ 2 grey tea bags
→ 1 low fat Greek yogurt pot
→ A teaspoon of ground cinnamon

DIRECTIONS

1. First, peel the 2 mangoes, remove the central stones, wash them, dry them, and leave them half parts whole.
2. Put 1 cup and ½ of water and the grey tea bags in the base of the steamer.
3. Bring the water to a boil.
4. Put the half mangoes in the steamer basket and when the water starts to boil, put the mangoes to cook for 20 minutes.
5. After the cooking time, remove the basket and let the mangoes cool.
6. Meanwhile, put the low-fat Greek yogurt and cinnamon in a bowl and with a fork mix and mix well.
7. Put the yogurt sauce on the bottom of the serving dish and put the mango on top and serve.

NUTRITIONAL VALUES:

Calories	Protein	Carbs	Fat	Fiber	Sodium	Sugar	Cholesterol
183	12 gr	24 gr	6 gr	5 gr	8 mg	18 gr	0 mg

VANILLA AND COCOA PANNA COTTA

PREPARATION TIME: 25 minutes

SERVINGS: 2

INGREDIENTS

→ 1 cup of skimmed milk
→ 2 gelatin sheets
→ 1 tbsp of unsweetened cocoa powder
→ 1 tbsp of cane sugar
→ 1 tsp of raw honey
→ A vanilla pod

DIRECTIONS

1. You can start by putting the gelatin sheets to soak in cold water for 10 minutes.
2. Meanwhile, put the skimmed milk in a saucepan along with the sugar and honey.
3. Leave a little skimmed milk on one side to mix the gelatin later.
4. Heat over low heat, stirring constantly.
5. As soon as the cream comes to a boil, remove it from the heat and add gelatin.
6. Also add cocoa powder and vanilla and mix well.
7. Before it comes to a boil, remove it from the heat, and pour in the well-squeezed gelatin.
8. Add the rest of the skimmed milk that you had set aside, and mix well, to mix the jelly.
9. Pour the panna cotta into 2 aluminum cups and put it to rest in the fridge for at least 6 hours.
10. As soon as it is time to serve the panna cotta, put very hot water in a container and immerse the bottom of the cups for a few seconds.
11. Then take them and turn them upside down on a serving dish.
12. You can serve this dessert.

NUTRITIONAL VALUES:

Calories	Protein	Carbs	Fat	Fiber	Sodium	Sugar	Cholesterol
101	5 gr	21 gr	1 gr	4 gr	43 mg	16 gr	2 mg

SNACK RECIPES

APRICOT AND OAT FLAKES YOGURT

PREPARATION TIME: **10 minutes**

SERVINGS: **2**

INGREDIENTS

→ ½ cup of low-fat white Greek yogurt
→ 2 apricots
→ The grated rind of an orange
→ 1 tsp of ground cinnamon
→ 2 tbsp of oat flakes

DIRECTIONS

1. As the first operation, peel, wash and dry the apricots, cut them in half, remove the stone and cut them into cubes.
2. Put the apricots in a bowl and add the orange zest and 1 tsp of ground cinnamon.
3. Stir to flavor the apricots well.
4. Add the yogurt and mix until everything is well blended.
5. Now put the mixture in two bowls.
6. Sprinkle with 1 tbsp of oat flakes for each bowl and serve.

NUTRITIONAL VALUES:

Calories	Protein	Carbs	Fat	Fiber	Sodium	Sugar	Cholesterol
161	6 gr	27 gr	4 gr	4 gr	28 mg	20 gr	0 mg

BANANA AND VANILLA VEGAN SMOOTHIE

PREPARATION TIME: 10 minutes

SERVINGS: 2

INGREDIENTS

→ 1 ripe banana
→ 1 glass of unsweetened vegetable milk
→ 1 vanilla pod
→ 1 tsp of honey

DIRECTIONS

1. Slice the banana, wash it, and then cut the pulp into small pieces.
2. Put the banana pieces, vegetable milk and honey in the blender glass.
3. Cut the vanilla pod in half and add the seeds to the other ingredients.
4. Blend everything at high speed, to get a homogeneous and smooth mixture.
5. Put the banana vegan smoothie in the glasses, add two straws and serve.

NUTRITIONAL VALUES:

Calories	Protein	Carbs	Fat	Fiber	Sodium	Sugar	Cholesterol
103	4 gr	20 gr	2 gr	5 gr	51 mg	12 gr	0 mg

COCOA STRAWBERRY AND YOGURT SNACK

PREPARATION TIME: 2 minutes

SERVINGS: 2

INGREDIENTS

→ ½ cup of strawberries
→ 4 crumbled walnuts
→ 1 cup of low-fat Greek yogurt
→ 2 tsp of unsweetened cocoa powder

DIRECTIONS

1. First, operation, wash and rinse the straw-berries well.
2. Put the low-fat yogurt divided into two parts into two separate bowls.
3. Add the coarsely chopped walnuts, and strawberries, and sprinkle everything with bitter cocoa.
4. You can serve this snack.

NUTRITIONAL VALUES:

Calories	Protein	Carbs	Fat	Fiber	Sodium	Sugar	Cholesterol
150	6 gr	15 gr	9 gr	5 gr	49 mg	8 gr	0 mg

MANGO AND TUNA HARD-BOILED EGGS

PREPARATION TIME: 25 minutes
SERVINGS: 2

INGREDIENTS

- 2 eggs
- 1 tbsp of low sodium mustard
- Half a mango
- ¼ cup of low sodium natural canned tuna
- 1 tsp of chopped parsley

DIRECTIONS

1. You can start by preparing the eggs. Put a saucepan full of water to boil. As soon as it starts to boil, add the eggs, and cook for 10 minutes.
2. After 10 minutes, put the eggs to cool with cold water and then peel them. Halve them, separate the yolks from the whites and put the yolks in a bowl.
3. Peel the half mango. Remove the stone, wash it, and then dry it.
4. Put the mango in a mixer together with the drained low sodium tuna and mustard and chop until you get a homogeneous mixture.
5. Add the mango and tuna mix to the egg yolks and mix everything with a fork.
6. Take a few bags, put the egg yolk mix inside, and fill the inside of the egg whites.
7. Serve sprinkled with chopped parsley.

NUTRITIONAL VALUES:

Calories	Protein	Carbs	Fat	Fiber	Sodium	Sugar	Cholesterol
207	16 gr	15 gr	9 gr	4 gr	6 mg	10 gr	80 mg

PEACH AND GINGER VEGAN SMOOTHIE

PREPARATION TIME: 10 minutes

SERVINGS: 2

INGREDIENTS

→ 2 little peaches
→ 2 little oranges
→ 1 tbsp of fresh minces ginger
→ 1 cup of unsweetened coconut milk
→ 1 pinch of cinnamon

DIRECTIONS

1. Peel and wash the peaches and then cut them into small pieces.
2. Wash and dry the ginger, then mince it.
3. Squeeze the oranges and strain the juice into the blender glass.
4. Add the peach pieces, unsweetened coconut milk, cinnamon, and ginger.
5. Blend everything at high speed, to get a smooth and homogeneous mixture.
6. Put the vegan smoothie in glasses, add some ice cubes and serve.

NUTRITIONAL VALUES:

Calories	Protein	Carbs	Fat	Fiber	Sodium	Sugar	Cholesterol
133	4 gr	28 gr	3 gr	6 gr	72 mg	20 gr	0 mg

PINEAPPLE AND LOW SODIUM COOKED HAM CROUTONS

PREPARATION TIME: 15 minutes

SERVINGS: 2

INGREDIENTS

→ 2 slices of wholemeal bread of 0.11 lbs for each
→ 1/3 cup of low-fat white Greek yogurt
→ 4 slices of pineapple
→ ½ tsp of chopped mint
→ ½ cup of low sodium and low-fat cooked ham
→ A pinch of salt and pepper

DIRECTIONS

1. First, wash and dry the pineapple slices.
2. Heat a grill and toast the slices of bread for 1/2 minutes per side.
3. Remove the slices of bread and grill the pineapple slices, always a couple of minutes on each side.
4. Put the bread on the serving plates.
5. Place the low sodium ham and then the pineapple slices on top of each slice of bread.
6. Put a few tablespoons of low-fat Greek yogurt on top, sprinkle with the washed and chopped mint and serve.

NUTRITIONAL VALUES:

Calories	Protein	Carbs	Fat	Fiber	Sodium	Sugar	Cholesterol
257	21 gr	38 gr	4 gr	5 gr	345 mg	18 gr	30 mg

SMOKED SALMON STUFFED AVOCADO

PREPARATION TIME: 20 minutes

SERVINGS: 2

INGREDIENTS

→ 1 ripe little avocado

→ 1/3 cup of smoked salmon

→ 2 bay leaves

→ 1 tbsp of low sodium and low-fat yogurt sauce

→ Half an orange

→ 1 tsp of Olive oil

→ 1 tsp of chopped chives

→ A pinch of salt

DIRECTIONS

1. Start by washing and drying the bay leaves and orange.

2. Squeeze a bit of orange juice.

3. In the meantime, peel the avocado, remove the stone, wash it, and dry it.

4. Put the smoked salmon cut into pieces in a bowl, add sage, orange juice, yogurt sauce and olive oil and mix everything.

5. Fill each half of the avocados with the salmon and yogurt sauce mixture decorated with chopped chives and serve.

NUTRITIONAL VALUES:

Calories	Protein	Carbs	Fat	Fiber	Sodium	Sugar	Cholesterol
188	11 gr	8 gr	18 gr	6 gr	319 mg	2 gr	10 mg

TURKEY AND DILL OMELET

PREPARATION TIME: 25 minutes

SERVINGS: 2

INGREDIENTS

→ 3 eggs (2 white eggs and 1 whole egg)
→ ¼ cup of low sodium roasted turkey
→ 1 tsp of dried dill
→ 1 tsp of chives
→ Olive oil to taste
→ A pinch of salt and pepper

DIRECTIONS

1. The first thing to do is to take a bowl and put the eggs inside. Start whipping the eggs with the help of a manual whisk.
2. Wash the chives and chop them.
3. Add the dill and chives, a pinch of salt and pepper, and continue whisking.
4. Chop the roasted turkey and put it in the bowl with the eggs.
5. Gently mix the turkey and eggs with a fork.
6. Take a non-stick pan and heat the olive oil.
7. Pour in the eggs and cook for 10 minutes, covering the pan with a lid.
8. Move the pan from time to time to prevent the omelet from sticking to the edges.
9. After 10 minutes, using the lid or a plate, turn the omelet and cook, still covered, for another 5 minutes
10. As soon as cooking is finished, serve the turkey and dill omelet immediately, directly on serving plates.

NUTRITIONAL VALUES:

Calories	Protein	Carbs	Fat	Fiber	Sodium	Sugar	Cholesterol
219	19 gr	4 gr	12 gr	1 gr	61 mg	2 gr	300 mg

TOFU AND TOMATO-STUFFED LETTUCE LEAVES

PREPARATION TIME: 25 minutes

SERVINGS: 2

INGREDIENTS

→ 5 large leaves of romaine lettuce
→ 1/3 cup of diced tofu
→ 4 cherry tomatoes
→ 2 tsp of low sodium mustard
→ 2 tsp of apple cider vinegar
→ A pinch of salt

DIRECTIONS

1. As the first, step, wash the lettuce leaves and dry them. Finely chop 1 lettuce leaf and set the other 4 aside.
2. Wash and dry the cherry tomatoes and then cut them into small cubes.
3. Rinse and dice tofu cheese.
4. Now put the tofu cheese, chopped lettuce and cherry tomatoes in the bowl with the chopped eggs.
5. Add the tuna and apple cider vinegar and mix everything. Add the low sodium mustard, and a pinch of salt and mix all the ingredients.
6. Now take the whole lettuce leaves and stuff them with the tofu and tomato filling, placing them in such a way that they look like a kind of bowl.
7. You can serve this snack.

NUTRITIONAL VALUES:

Calories	Protein	Carbs	Fat	Fiber	Sodium	Sugar	Cholesterol
122	6 gr	10 gr	7 gr	5 gr	14 mg	4 gr	0 mg

YOGURT PISTACHIO AND EGG WHITE MUFFINS

PREPARATION TIME: 30 minutes

SERVINGS: 2

INGREDIENTS

→ ½ cup of egg white
→ ¼ cup of low-fat Greek yogurt
→ 1 tbsp of chopped pistachios
→ ¼ cup of oat flour
→ 1 tsp of raw honey

DIRECTIONS

1. First, heat the oven to 338°F.
2. In a bowl, whisk the ½ cup of egg white until stiff.
3. Whip them until the mixture sticks to the bowl.
4. Add the low-fat Greek yogurt to the eggs and mix gently.
5. Add the oat flour and honey, stirring again carefully.
6. With the help of an electric whisk or a fork, go to mix the mixture until you get a homogeneous but slightly liquid mixture.
7. Now take the muffin molds and with a spoon (or ladle) pour some dough.
8. Add pieces of pistachios to the center of the dough and cover everything with more dough.
9. Bake the healthy muffins and cook for 20 minutes.
10. Once they are ready, let them cool.
11. Serve these pistachio, egg white and yogurt muffins warm.

NUTRITIONAL VALUES:

Calories	Protein	Carbs	Fat	Fiber	Sodium	Sugar	Cholesterol
237	14 gr	16 gr	11 gr	4 gr	36 mg	7 gr	5 mg

Meal Plan 1-7

	Breakfast	Lunch	Dinner	Snack
Mon	Artichokes creamy omelet	Cashew and low-fat cheese stuffed peppers	Tofu and sweet potato stuffed eggplant	Apricot and oat flakes yogurt
Tue	Peach hazelnut and berries yogurt bowl	Chicken and peppers parsley Black rice	Pecans and turmeric zucchini cream	Cocoa strawberry and yogurt snack
Wen	Rice cocoa and honey pancake	Green tea and ginger clam soup	Low fat cheese and tomato stuffed pepper	Almond and lemon cake
Wed	Strawberry and avocado toast	Scallops and zucchini rice	Peppers and orange halibut	Cranberry and cottage cheesecake
Thu	Zucchini and tuna scrambled eggs	Spicy chicken and shallot stew	Fennel and basil cod	Passion fruit and oat flakes yogurt dessert
Sat	Avocado almond and pistachio cheesy pancake	Peas and mushroom cod stew	Spicy chicken and shallot stew	Tea and yogurt sauce mango
Sun	Banana and honey pancake	Celery and Carrots chicken	Steamed herbs salmon and cucumbers mint salad	Vanilla and cocoa panna cotta

Meal Plan 8-14

	Breakfast	Lunch	Dinner	Snack
Mon	Artichokes creamy omelet	Tofu and sweet potato stuffed eggplant	Cashew and low-fat cheese stuffed peppers	Apricot and oat flakes yogurt
Tue	Cocoa strawberry and yogurt snack	Chicken and peppers parsley Black rice	Peas and mushroom cod stew	Almond and lemon cake
Wen	Rice cocoa and honey pancake	Fennel and basil cod	Low fat cheese and tomato stuffed pepper	Peach hazelnut and berries yogurt bowl
Wed	Vanilla and cocoa panna cotta	Scallops and zucchini rice	Spicy chicken and shallot stew	Cranberry and cottage cheesecake
Thu	Passion fruit and oat flakes yogurt dessert	Peppers and orange halibut	Green tea and ginger clam soup	Zucchini and tuna scrambled eggs
Sat	Avocado almond and pistachio cheesy pancake	Pecans and turmeric zucchini cream	Celery and Carrots chicken	Banana and honey pancake
Sun	Tea and yogurt sauce mango	Spicy chicken and shallot stew	Steamed herbs salmon and cucumbers mint salad	Strawberry and avocado toast

Meal Plan 15-21

	Breakfast	Lunch	Dinner	Snack
Mon	Artichokes creamy omelet	Cashew and low-fat cheese stuffed peppers	Spicy chicken and shallot stew	Apricot and oat flakes yogurt
Tue	Vanilla and cocoa panna cotta	Spicy chicken and shallot stew	Fennel and basil cod	Cocoa strawberry and yogurt snack
Wen	Avocado almond and pistachio cheesy pancake	Celery and Carrots chicken	Low fat cheese and tomato stuffed pepper	Almond and lemon cake
Wed	Strawberry and avocado toast	Scallops and zucchini rice	Tofu and sweet potato stuffed eggplant	Zucchini and tuna scrambled eggs
Thu	Cranberry and cottage cheesecake	Chicken and peppers parsley Black rice	Pecans and turmeric zucchini cream	Passion fruit and oat flakes yogurt dessert
Sat	Rice cocoa and honey pancake	Peas and mushroom cod stew	Peppers and orange halibut	Banana and honey pancake
Sun	Tea and yogurt sauce mango	Steamed herbs salmon and cucumbers mint salad	Green tea and ginger clam soup	Peach hazelnut and berries yogurt bowl

Meal Plan 22-28

	Breakfast	Lunch	Dinner	Snack
Mon	Artichokes creamy omelet	Cashew and low-fat cheese stuffed peppers	Tofu and sweet potato stuffed eggplant	Apricot and oat flakes yogurt
Tue	Peach hazelnut and berries yogurt bowl	Chicken and peppers parsley Black rice	Pecans and turmeric zucchini cream	Cocoa strawberry and yogurt snack
Wen	Almond and lemon cake	Low fat cheese and tomato stuffed pepper	Green tea and ginger clam soup	Rice cocoa and honey pancake
Wed	Strawberry and avocado toast	Fennel and basil cod	Peppers and orange halibut	Cranberry and cottage cheesecake
Thu	Zucchini and tuna scrambled eggs	Spicy chicken and shallot stew	Scallops and zucchini rice	Passion fruit and oat flakes yogurt dessert
Sat	Tea and yogurt sauce mango	Peas and mushroom cod stew	Spicy chicken and shallot stew	Avocado almond and pistachio cheesy pancake
Sun	Banana and honey pancake	Celery and Carrots chicken	Steamed herbs salmon and cucumbers mint salad	Vanilla and cocoa panna cotta